long

u

Sounds & Letters (22)

KNOWLEDGE BOOKS

fruit	cube
tube	blue
juice	ruler
flute	

u

fruit

cube

5

tube

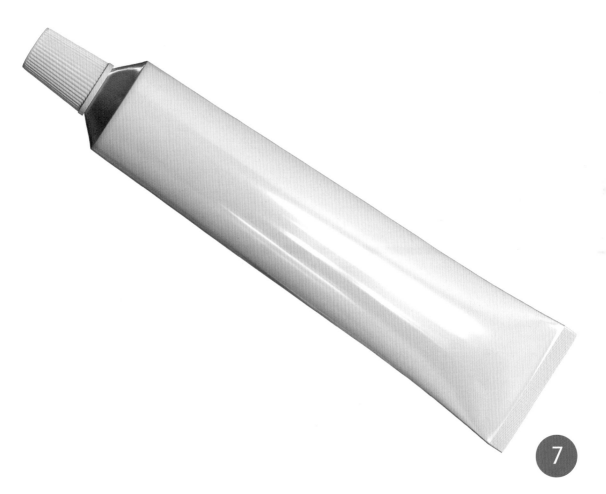

7

blue

juice

11

ruler

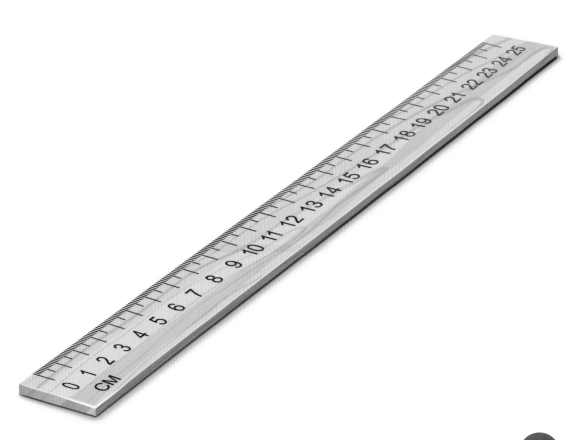

13

flute

15

fruit	cube
tube	blue
juice	ruler
flute	

Knowledge Books and Software

PO Box 50 Sandgate, Queensland 4017 Australia
p. +617-55680288 f. +617-55680277 email: sales@kbs.com.au

First Published 2022
ISBN 9781922516947
Text and editing: Carole Crimeen
Design and layout: Suzanne Fletcher
Publisher: Robert Watts

Series Information: **Sounds and Letters**

Reproduction and Communication for educational purposes
Fair Go!
Make sure you record any copying of this book so we may get some benefit please.
The Australian Copyright Act 1968 (the Act) allows a maximum of one chapter or 10% of the pages of this work, whichever is the greater, to be reproduced and/or communicated by any educational institution for its educational purposed provided that the educational institution (or the body that administers it) has given a renumeration notice to the Copyright Agency Limited (CAL) under the Act.
For details of the CAL licence for educational institutions contact:
Copyright Agency Limited
Level 15, 233 Castlereagh Street,
SYDNEY, NSW 2000
Telephone: +61293947600 Fax: +61293947601 Email: info@copyright.com.au
Reproduction and Communication for other purposes
Except as permitted under the Act (for example for the services of the Crown or in reliance on one of the fair dealing exceptions ie. a fair dealing for the purposes of research or study) no part of this book may be reproduced, stored in a retrieval system, communicated or transmitted in any form or by any means without prior written permission.

Credits

Photographs: Cover © wee dezign; p. 1 © djmilic, Supertrooper, Pixel-Shot, Katrine Glazkova; p. 3 © CHALERMCHAI99; p. 5 © DnD-Production.com; p. 7 © 3d_hokage; p. 11 © Lotus_studio; p. 13 © Aleksangel; p. 15 © Valentin Valkov/Shutterstock.

Phonic support books are a wonderful resource for emergent readers as they encourage independent reading and help students make the link between letters and the sounds they represent.

Have students identify the images on the title page to listen for the long or short vowel sound that they will hear through the book.

Encourage students to point to each word as they read through the book.

ISBN: 9781922516947

9 781922 516947

KNOWLEDGE
BOOKS

Sounds&
Letters